We give tha[nks to the One] above, for friends [and fam,]
life and love. For sun
and moon and all the stars,
for all we can be and
all we are. And for...

SAYING GRACE

~

SAYING GRACE

BLESSINGS *for the* FAMILY TABLE

Edited by SARAH McELWAIN

Illustrations by DAVID DEAN

CHRONICLE BOOKS
SAN FRANCISCO

Library of Congress Cataloging-in-Publication Data available.

ISBN 0-8118-4025-5

Manufactured in China.

Designed by Susanne Weihl

Distributed in Canada by Raincoast Books
9050 Shaughnessy Street
Vancouver, British Columbia V6P 6E5

10 9 8 7 6 5 4 3 2 1

Chronicle Books LLC
85 Second Street
San Francisco, California 94105

www.chroniclebooks.com

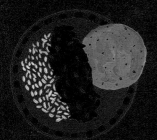
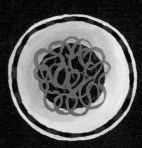

SAYING GRACE

Expressing gratitude for the food on our tables is universal. People in all times and in every place have felt the need to say thanks for what they are about to eat. Whether graces are said over meals eaten with chopsticks or spoons, around a campfire, or over the best holiday dishes, they are part of every culture.

The graces and table blessings in *Saying Grace* are like stuffing recipes. There are many different kinds, and everyone has a favorite. Some, like celery, onion, and bread crumbs, are simply traditional. Passed from one generation to another and repeated daily or yearly at holidays, they are as familiar at the table as the traditional foods they share. Other blessings in *Saying Grace* are exotic, like recipes that call for unusual fruits and spices.

The graces found here are drawn from a variety of great religious books and connect us to our ancient pasts. Some are regional. Like a recipe for Louisiana Crayfish Jambalaya stuffing, they evoke a certain time and place. The ceremonial Native American corn-planting chants, for example, take us for a moment to the early American Great Plains, while 17th-century fishermen's prayers hark back to the rugged coast of Scotland.

Most blessings collected in *Saying Grace* address some form of the sacred, but also included are those like the "cowboy blessings" and "singing graces" that say thanks in a slightly more irreverent and humorous manner.

All of the selections are intended to inspire thoughts of gratitude. Many traditions call for spontaneous expressions of thankfulness spoken by those present around the table. Others simply sit together in a moment of shared, silent thankfulness.

Since many of the world's greatest writers, poets, humanitarians, and philosophers have composed poems or words of gratitude for their daily bread, *Saying Grace* includes quotations from St. Francis of Assisi; Zoroaster, the late 7th century Persian philosopher; Josephine Delphine Henderson Heard, the African-American poet; and Dorothy Day, cofounder of the Catholic Worker movement.

A number of the entries are anonymous—blessing and graces that have outlasted our knowledge of their authors. Much research was done in the compiling of this book to trace the origins of these blessings, but in many cases their sources may no longer be available. Some, like the proverbs—sayings that express generally accepted observations on human behavior—could arguably be attributed to many different sources.

Saying Grace is an eclectic collection of graces and food blessings from different centuries, cultures, and geographic locations. Intended for holidays and every day, it can be passed around the table or enjoyed silently, opened every night or whenever the spirit moves you.

Hail, hail, hail.

May happiness come.

May meat come,

May corn come,

Just as the farmers work,

And look forward to the reaping.

So may we sit again as we are sitting now.

PRAYER OF THE GA, GHANA

Think, and thank God.

PROVERB

––––––––––––––

Father, we thank Thee for this food,
For health and strength and all things good.
May others all these blessings share,
And hearts be grateful everywhere.

TRADITIONAL AMERICAN BLESSING,
CIRCA 1800s

For each new morning with its light,

For rest and shelter of the night,

For health and food,

For love and friends,

For everything Thy goodness sends.

RALPH WALDO EMERSON (1803–1882),
AMERICAN ESSAYIST

Without Thy sunshine and Thy rain,
We would not have the golden grain;
Without Thy love we'd not be fed;
We thank Thee for our daily bread.

ANONYMOUS

Great God accept our gratitude,

For the great gifts on us bestowed—

For raiment, shelter, and for food.

Great God, our gratitude we bring,

Accept our humble offering,

For all the gifts on us bestowed,

Thy name be evermore adored.

JOSEPHINE DELPHINE HENDERSON HEARD
(1861–1921), AFRICAN-AMERICAN POET,
DOXOLOGY

Though our mouths were full of song as the sea,

And our tongues of exultation as the multitude
of its waves,

And our lips of praise as the wide-extended
firmament;

Though our eyes shone with light like the sun
and the moon,

And our hands were spread forth like the eagles
of heaven,

And our feet were swift as hinds, we should still
be unable

To thank thee and bless Thy name.

O Lord our God and God of our fathers, for one
thousandth

or one ten-thousandth of the bounties which
Thou has bestowed

Upon our fathers and upon us.

THE HEBREW PRAYER BOOK

Blessed are we who can laugh at ourselves,
For we shall never cease to be amused.

ANONYMOUS

———————

Now this day,
My sun father,
Now that you have come out standing to your
    sacred place,
That from which we draw the water of life,
Prayer meal,
Here I give to you.
Your long life,
Your old age,
Your waters,
Your seeds,
Your riches,
Your power,
Your strong spirit,
All these to me may you grant.

ZUÑI PRAYER

This ritual is One.

The food is One.

We who offer the food are One.

The fire of hunger is also One.

All action is One.

We who understand this are One.

HINDU BLESSING

Been out on the range,
All dusty and tired.
Been ridin' and ropin' all day,
Around the chuck wagon.

We bow down our heads,
And sing out the cowboys' grace.
Allelujah, Amen, Amen.
Allelujah, Amen, Amen.

A COWBOY GRACE

Make a joyful noise unto the Lord, all the lands!

Serve the Lord with gladness!

Come into His presence with singing!

Know that the Lord is God!

It is He that made us, and we are His;

We are His people, and the sheep of His pasture.

Enter His gates with thanksgiving,

And His courts with praise!

Give thanks to Him, bless His name!

For the Lord is good;

His steadfast love endures forever,

And His faithfulness to all generations.

PSALM 100

Soup and fish explain half the emotions in life.

SYDNEY SMITH (1771–1845),
ENGLISH CLERGYMAN AT
ST. PAUL'S CATHEDRAL, LONDON

Praise to God who giveth meat,

Convenient unto all who eat.

Praise for tea and buttered toast,

Father, Son, and Holy Ghost.

SCOTTISH GRACE

May the abundance of this table
Never fail and never be less,
Thanks to the blessings of God,
Who has satisfied our needs.
To Him be the glory forever.
Amen.

ARMENIAN GRACE, LEBANON

Oh Lord, now bless and bind us.

And put old Satan 'hind us.

Oh let your spirit mind us.

Don't let none hungry find us.

BLESSING WITH COMPANY PRESENT,
AFRICAN-AMERICAN FOLK RHYME,
18TH CENTURY

Turkey boiled is turkey spoiled;

And turkey roast is turkey lost.

But for turkey braised,

The Lord be praised.

ANONYMOUS

A table is not blessed if it has fed no scholars.

YIDDISH PROVERB

———————

For these and all Thy blessings so kindly
bestowed upon us, our most sincere
thanks, dear Ahura Mazda.

ZOROASTER, LATE 7TH TO
EARLY 6TH CENTURY, B.C.,
GRACE AT MEAL TIMES

———————

Lord Jesus, be our guest;
Our morning joy, our evening rest.
And with our daily bread, and part,
Bring peace and joy to every heart.
Amen.

TRADITIONAL AMERICAN GRACE

Time is

Too slow for those who wait,

Too swift for those who fear,

Too long for those who grieve,

Too short for those who rejoice,

But for those who love,

Time is eternity.

Hours fly, flowers die,

New days, new ways pass by,

Love stays.

HENRY VAN DYKE (1852–1933),
AMERICAN CLERGYMAN AND WRITER
(found on a sundial at the
University of Virginia)

O you who believe!

Eat of the good things that we have provided

for you, and be grateful to Allah.

It is He you worship.

ISLAMIC PRAYER

God has two dwellings:

One in heaven, and the other

in a meek and thankful heart.

IZAAK WALTON (1593–1683),
ENGLISH BIOGRAPHER AND AUTHOR

Lord, bless this food

Before we eat.

Bless Thou the bread,

And bless the meat.

Amen.

ANONYMOUS

For peaceful homes, and healthful days,

For all the blessings Earth displays,

We owe Thee thankfulness and praise,

Giver of all!

CHRISTOPHER WADSWORTH (1807–1885),
ANGLICAN BISHOP

All my soul is in delight,

When Mommy fixes kraut just right.

FROM AN EARLY
PENNSYLVANIA DUTCH SONG

They that have no other meat,
Bread and butter are glad to eat.

JOHN RAY (1627–1705).
ENGLISH NATURALIST
AND COLLECTOR OF PROVERBS

32

O Lord, bless the waters of the river.

Gladden the face of the earth.

May her furrows be watered, her fruits multiply;

Prepare it for seed and harvest.

EGYPTIAN PRAYER
FOR THE RISING OF THE NILE

Heaven,

Please make the rain fall,

So I have water to drink;

So I may plow my rice field;

So I may have my bowl of rice;

And my fish in great slices.

VIETNAMESE FARMERS' PRAYER

Anticipate the good so that you may enjoy it.

———————————

How beautiful and perfect are the animals!
How perfect the Earth, and the minutest thing
    on it!
What is called good is perfect, and what is
    called bad is just as perfect;
The vegetables and minerals are all perfect,
    and the imponderable fluids perfect.
Slowly and surely they have pass'd on to this,
    and slowly and surely they yet pass on.
I swear I think there is nothing but immortality.

God is great!

God is good!

Let us thank Him

For our food.

Amen.

TRADITIONAL AMERICAN GRACE

Olodumare, oh Divine One!
I give thanks to You,
The one who is as near as my heartbeat,
And more anticipated than my next breath.
Let Your wisdom become one with this vessel,
As I lift my voice in thanks for Your love.

YORUBAN BLESSING

There is enough in the world for everyone
to have plenty to live on happily and to be at
peace with his neighbors.

HARRY S. TRUMAN (1884–1972),
33RD U.S. PRESIDENT

Grub first, then ethics.

BERTOLT BRECHT (1898–1956),
GERMAN WRITER

This night I hold an old accustom'd feast,

Whereto I have invited many a guest,

Such as I love; and you among them the store,

One more, most welcome, makes my

numbers more.

WILLIAM SHAKESPEARE (1564–1616),
ROMEO AND JULIET, ACT 1, SC. 2, LINE 20

39

Lord most giving and resourceful, I implore you;
Make it your will that this people enjoy
The goods and riches you naturally give,
That naturally issue from you,
That are pleasing and savory,
That delight and comfort,
Though lasting but briefly,
Passing away as if in a dream.

AZTEC PRAYER, CIRCA 1500s

Eat your bread with joy;
Drink your wine with a merry heart.

ECCLESIASTES 9:7

Prevail on each god to give us his bounty!
Now at your appealing import to us the charm
Of pleasant voices and for our own uplift.
Preserve us evermore, O gods, with your blessing!

BHAGAVAD GITA, HINDU BLESSING

To be said while holding hands:

May the love that is in my heart
pass from my hand to yours.

TRADITIONAL AMERICAN GRACE

44

Before me, may it be delightful.
Behind me, may it be delightful.
Around me, may it be delightful.
Below me, may it be delightful.
Above me, may it be delightful.
All, may it be delightful.

NAVAJO PRAYER

Praised are You, Adonai our God,
    Guide of the Universe,
Who creates innumerable living beings
    and their needs, for all the things
You have created to sustain every living being.
Praised are You, the life of the Universe.

JEWISH BLESSING

45

May the longtime sun shine
Upon you, all love surround you,
And the sweet light within you
Guide you on your way.

TRADITIONAL IRISH BLESSING

Do good and don't look back.

DUTCH PROVERB

————————————

May the blessing of God rest upon you,
May his peace abide within you,
May his presence illuminate your heart,
Now and forevermore.

SUFI BLESSING

May there always be work for your hands to do;
May your purse always hold a coin or two;
May the sun always shine upon your windowpane;
May a rainbow be certain to follow each rain;
May the hand of a friend always be near to you, and
May God fill your heart with gladness to cheer you.

IRISH BLESSING

When eating bamboo shoots,
remember the man who planted them.

CHINESE PROVERB

Now that I am about to eat, O Great Spirit,
Give my thanks to the beasts and birds
Whom you have provided for my hunger;
And pray deliver my sorrow
That living things must make a sacrifice
    for my comfort and well-being.
Let the feather of corn spring up in its time
And let it not wither but make full grains
For the fires of our cooking pots,
Now that I am about to eat.

NATIVE AMERICAN GRACE

Bless this food we are about to receive.

Give bread to those who hunger,

And hunger for justice to us who have bread.

Amen.

TRADITIONAL AMERICAN GRACE

―――――――

Be present at our table, Lord;

Be here, and everywhere adored;

Thy mercies bless and grant that we

May feast in fellowship with Thee.

Amen.

ANONYMOUS

―――――――

Round the table;

Peace and joy prevail.

May all who share

This season's delight

Enjoy countless more.

CHINESE BLESSING

Bless us, O Lord, and these Thy gifts which we
are about to receive
From Thy bounty, through Christ our Lord.
Amen.

(same quote in Latin)

Benedic, Domine, nos et haec tua dona quae de
tua largitate sumus sumpturi. Per Christum
Dominum nostrum.
Amen.

TRADITIONAL CATHOLIC PRAYER
BEFORE MEALS

Hold on to what is good

    even if it is a handful of earth.

Hold on to what you believe

    even if it is a tree that stands by itself.

Hold on to what you must do

    even if it is a long way from here.

Hold on to life

    even when it is easier letting go.

Hold on to my hand

    even when I have gone away from you.

PUEBLO VERSE

Rub-a-dub-dub,

Thanks for the grub.

Yea, God!

ANONYMOUS

———————

Bless us O Lord, for these gifts

we are about to receive from your bounty.

TRADITIONAL CHRISTIAN GRACE,
CIRCA 1800s

Everyone at the table join hands
for a silent moment.

QUAKER GRACE

In plenty think of want; in want,
do not presume on plenty.

CHINESE PROVERB

That is perfect. This is perfect.
Perfect comes from perfect.
Take perfect from perfect,
The remainder is perfect.
May peace and peace and
Peace be everywhere.

THE UPANISHADS, SACRED HINDU TEXT,
CIRCA 2500 B.C.

Bless these Thy gifts, most gracious God,
From whom all goodness springs;
Make clean our hearts and feed our souls,
With good and joyful things.

TRADITIONAL CHRISTIAN GRACE

The custom of saying grace at meals had, probably, its origin in the early times of the world, and the hunter-state of man, when dinners were precarious things, and a full meal was something more than a common blessing; when a bellyful was a windfall, and looked like a special providence.

CHARLES LAMB (1775–1834),
ENGLISH ESSAYIST, *GRACE BEFORE MEAT*

Gracias, arigato, merci beaucoup.

(clap clap)

Gracias, arigato, merci beaucoup.

(clap clap)

I can say thank you to God

(clap clap)

in Spanish, Japanese, French words, too.

(clap clap)

CHILDREN'S RHYME

Aloha to God above.
Aloha, a word that means
I love you.
Mahalo, too, means
I thank you.
Mahalo, aloha to God.
(Ma/ha/low)

HAWAIIAN GRACE

So I may raise corn,

So I may raise beans,

So I may raise wheat,

So I may raise squash,

So that with all good fortune I may be blessed.

PUEBLO BLESSING

Give me a good digestion, Lord,
And also something to digest.
Give me a healthy body, Lord,
With sense to keep it at its best.

Give me a healthy mind, Lord,
To keep the good and pure in sight;
Which, seeing sin, is not appalled,
But finds a way to set it right.

Give me a mind that is not bored,
That does not whimper, whine, or sigh.
Don't let me worry overmuch
About the fussy thing called "I."

Give me a sense of humor, Lord;
Give me the grace to see a joke;
To get some happiness from life,
And pass it on to other folk.

A PRAYER FOUND
IN CHESTER CATHEDRAL,
CIRCA 1850

62

Heavenly Father, bless us
And keep us all alive,
There's ten of us to dinner
And not enough for five.

ANONYMOUS

———————

Thou hast given so much to me . . .
Give me one thing more—
A grateful heart.

GEORGE HERBERT (1593–1633),
ENGLISH POET AND PASTOR

A haze on the far horizon,

The infinite, tender sky,

The ripe, rich tint of the cornfields,

And then wild geese sailing high—

All over upland and lowland

The charms of all the goldenrod—

Some of us call it autumn,

And others call it God.

WILLIAM HERBERT CARRUTH (1859–1924),
AMERICAN EDUCATOR

66

There's no joy in anything unless we share it.

AMERICAN PROVERB

For all that God in mercy sends,
For health and children, home and friends,
For comfort in the time of need,
For every kindly word and deed,
For happy thoughts and holy talk,
For guidance in our daily walk,
For everything give thanks!

For beauty in this world of ours,
For verdant grass and lovely flowers,
For song of birds, for hum of bees,
For refreshing summer breeze,
For hill and plain, for streams and wood,
For the great ocean's mighty flood.
For everything give thanks!

For sweet sleep which comes with night.
For the returning morning light,
For the bright sun that shines on high,
For the stars glittering in the sky,
For these and everything we see,
O Lord, our hearts we lift to Thee
For everything give thanks!

HELENA ISABELLA TUPPER (date unknown),
FOR EVERYTHING GIVE THANKS

Give strength, give thought, give deeds,
  give wealth;
Give love, give tears, and give thyself.
Give, give, be always giving;
Who gives not is not living.
The more you give, the more you live.

ANONYMOUS

The worship most acceptable to God
comes from a thankful and cheerful heart.

PLUTARCH (CIRCA A.D. 46–120),
GREEK BIOGRAPHER AND ESSAYIST

The Holy Supper is kept, indeed,

In what so we share with another's need;

Not what we give, but what we share,

For the gifts without the giver is bare;

Who gives himself with his alms feeds three:

Himself, his neighbor, and me.

JAMES RUSSELL LOWELL (1819–1891),
THE VISION OF SIR LAUNFOL

Praised be my Lord for our
Mother the Earth, which
Sustains us and keeps us and
Brings forth diverse fruits,
And flowers of many colors—
And grass.

ST. FRANCIS OF ASSISI (1181–1226),
THE CANTICLE OF THE CREATURES

Good bread,
Good meat;
Good God
Let's eat.

ANONYMOUS

71

May we be a channel of blessings,
For all that we meet.

EDGAR CAYCE (1877–1945),
AMERICAN PSYCHIC

Gratitude is the heart's memory.

ANONYMOUS

———————

Some hae meat, and canna eat,
And some wad eat that want it,
But we hae meat and we can eat,
And sae the Lord be thank it.

ROBERT BURNS (1759–1796),
SCOTLAND'S NATIONAL POET,
THE SELKIRK GRACE

———————

Gratitude is from the same root
    word as "grace," which signifies
    the free boundless mercy of God.
Thanksgiving is from the same root
    word as "think," so that to think
    is to thank.

WILLIS P. KING, *PULPIT PREACHING*
(date unknown)

As Thou has set the moon in the sky to be

    the poor man's lantern,

So let Thy light shine in my dark life

    and lighten my path;

As the rice is sown in the water,

And brings forth grain in great abundance,

    so let Thy word be sown in our

Midst that the harvest may be great;

    and as the banyan sends forth its

Branches to take root in our lives.

SOUTHERN INDIAN PRAYER,
SOURCE UNKNOWN

We cannot love God unless we love each other,

And to love each other we must know each other

In the breaking of bread and we are not alone

    anymore.

Heaven is a banquet and Life is a banquet, too,

Even with a crust, where there is companionship,

Love comes with community.

DOROTHY DAY (1897–1980),
COFOUNDER OF U.S. CATHOLIC
WORKER MOVEMENT

Lord behold our family here assembled.
We thank Thee for this place in which
We dwell, for the love that unites us, for
The peace accorded us this day, for the
Health, the work, the food, and the bright
Skies that make our lives delightful, for
Our friends in all parts of the earth.

Give us courage, gaiety, and the quiet mind.
Spare to us our friends, soften to us our enemies.
Bless us, if it may be, in all our innocent endeavors.
If it may not, give us the strength to encounter
    that which is to come.
May we be brave in peril, constant in tribulation,
    temperate in wrath,
And in all changes of fortune loyal and loving
    to one another.

ROBERT LOUIS STEVENSON (1850–1894),
SCOTTISH NOVELIST AND POET

Here's to those who love us,
And here's to those who don't.
A smile for those who are willing to,
And a tear for those who won't.

ANONYMOUS

From too much love of living,
From hope and fear set free,
We thank with brief Thanksgiving
Whatever gods may be.

ALGERNON CHARLES SWINBURNE
(1837–1909), *THE GARDEN OF PROSERPINE*

For flowers so beautiful and sweet,
For friends and clothes and food to eat,
For gracious hours, for work and play,
We thank Thee this Thanksgiving Day.

For father's care and mother's love,
For blue sky and clouds above.
For springtime and for autumn gay.
We thank Thee this Thanksgiving Day.

For all Thy gifts so good and fair,
Bestowed so freely everywhere.
Give us grateful hearts, we pray,
To thank Thee this Thanksgiving Day.

MATTIE M. RENWICK (1897–1920),
MICHIGAN POET

For All Thy Blessings,
For this new morning and its light,
The rest and shelter of the night,
For health and food, love and friends,
For every gift His goodness sends,
We thank Thee, gracious Lord.
Amen.

78

ANONYMOUS

The truths of the spirit are proved not by reasoning
  about them,
Or finding explanation of them, but only by acting
  upon them.
Their life is dependent upon what we do about them.
Mercy, gentleness, forgiveness, patience;
If we do not show them, they will cease to be.
Upon us depends the reality of God here on Earth
  today.

EDITH HAMILTON (1867–1963),
AMERICAN EDUCATOR AND GREEK SCHOLAR

79

Do all the good you can

By all the means you can,

In all ways you can,

In all places you can,

To all the people you can,

As long as ever you can.

JOHN WESLEY (1703–1791),
FOUNDER OF THE METHODISTS

Give us this day our daily bread.

MATTHEW 6:11

As the sun illuminates the moon and stars,
So let us illumine one another.

ANONYMOUS

A grateful thought toward Heaven
is a complete prayer.

GERMAN PROVERB

A crust eaten in peace is better
than a banquet partaken in anxiety.

AESOP (550 B.C.),
THE TOWN MOUSE AND THE COUNTRY MOUSE

What hymns are sung, what praises said,
For home-made miracles of bread.

LOUIS UNTERMEYER (1885–1978),
AMERICAN POET AND ANTHOLOGIST

For all things, and good, and true;
For all things that seemed not yet good yet
    turned to good;
For all the sweet compulsions of Thy will,
That chastened, tried, and wrought us to
    Thy shape;
For things unnumbered that we take of right,
And value first when they are withheld;

For light and air; sweet sense of sound and smell;
For ears to hear the heavenly harmonies;
For eyes to see the unseen in the seen;
For vision of the Wonder in the work;
For hearts to apprehend Thee everywhere;
We thank Thee, Lord.

JOHN OXENHAM (1861–1941),
ENGLISH POET, *THANKSGIVING*

84

Tune: "Yankee Doodle"

Thank you Lord for food and drink,
For warm and sunny weather,
Thank you Lord for all we have,
And that we're all together.
Thank you Lord for Jesus Christ,
Thanks for our salvation.
Thanks for dying on the cross,
For us and every nation. Amen.

GIRL SCOUT CAMPFIRE GRACE

Tune (can be done as a round):
"Row, Row, Row, Your Boat"

Thank, thank, thank you God.

Thank you now we pray.

You have given all we need,

To live through every day.

GIRL SCOUT CAMPFIRE GRACE

———————

Tune: "Rock Around the Clock"

God is great; God is good.

Let us thank Him for our food.

We're gonna thank the Lord in broad daylight.

We're gonna thank Him in the moon at night.

We're gonna thank our Lord for He is good!

   Amen.

GIRL SCOUT CAMPFIRE GRACE

Tune: "When Irish Eyes Are Smiling"

May the road rise up to meet you,
May the wind be at your back,
May good friends be there to greet you
And your table never lack.

May your life be filled with laughter,
And your heart be filled with song.
May God shine His light upon you,
As you live your whole life long.

TRADITIONAL IRISH BLESSING

Thank you for the world so sweet,
Thank you for the food we eat.
Thank you for the birds that sing,
Thank you God for everything.

CHILD'S BLESSING

Father, bless the food we take,

And bless us all for Jesus' sake.

Amen.

ANONYMOUS, *A SIMPLE GRACE*

———————

Reflect upon your present blessings,

Of which every man has plenty;

Not on your past misfortunes,

Of which all men have some.

CHARLES DICKENS (1812–1870),
ENGLISH WRITER

———————

I ain't what I wana be.

I ain't what I'm gona be.

But O Lord,

I ain't what I used to be.

AUTHOR OF *AN UNKNOWN SLAVE*
(date unknown)

To live content with small means; to seek
    elegance rather than luxury;
And refinement rather than fashion; to be
    worthy, not respectable;
And wealthy, not rich; to study hard, think
    quietly. talk gently,
Act frankly; to listen to stars and birds, to
    babes and sages, with open heart;
To bear all cheerfully, do all bravely, await
    occasion, hurry never; in a word,
To let the spiritual, unbidden, and unconscious
    grow up through the common.

This is to be my symphony.

WILLIAM ELLERY CHANNING (1780–1842),
AMERICAN UNITARIAN MINISTER,
MY SYMPHONY

May we walk with grace,

And may the light of the universe

Shine upon our path.

ANONYMOUS

How would it be,

If just for today,

We thought less about contests and rivalries,

Profits and politics,

Winners and sinners,

And more about

Helping and giving,

Mending and blending,

Reaching out,

And pitching in?

How would it be?

ANONYMOUS

91

———————

Quietly, easily, restfully, patiently,

serenely, peacefully, joyously, courageously,

confidently, trustfully

CHARLES R. BROWN (1862–1950),
AMERICAN CLERGYMAN AND EDUCATOR

To everything there is a season, and a time to
     every purpose under heaven:
A time to be born, and a time to die; a time to
     plant, and a time to pluck up that which
     is planted;
A time to kill, and a time to heal; a time to
     break down, and a time to build up;
A time to weep, and a time to laugh; a time to
     mourn, and a time to dance . . .
A time to rend, and a time to sew; a time to
     keep long silence, and a time to speak;
A time to love, and a time to hate; a time of
     war, and a time of peace.

ECCLESIASTES 3:1–4, 7–8

Without Thy sunshine and Thy rain,
We could not have the golden grain.
Without Thy love we'd not be fed;
We thank Thee for our daily bread.

ANONYMOUS

Consider your table as a table before the Lord:
chew well and hurry not.

ZOHAR, THE HEBREW BOOK OF SPLENDOR

The wealth of a man is the number
Of things which he loves and blesses,
And which he is loved and blessed by.

THOMAS CARLYLE (1795—1881),
ENGLISH WRITER

It's a beautiful world to see,
Or it's dismal in every zone.
The thing it must be in its gloom or its gleam,
Depends on yourself alone.

ANONYMOUS

We ought all to make an effort to act on our first thoughts and let our unspoken gratitude find expression. Then there will be more sunshine in the world, and more power to work for what is good.

ALBERT SCHWEITZER (1875–1965),
GERMAN MEDICAL MISSIONARY,
MEMORIES OF CHILDHOOD AND YOUTH

If there is righteousness in the heart,
There will be beauty in the character.
If there is beauty in the character,
There will be harmony in the home.
If there is harmony in the home,
There will be order in the nation.
When there is order in the nation,
There will be peace in the world.

CHINESE PROVERB

For food that stays our hunger,
For rest that brings us ease,
For homes where memories linger,
We give our thanks for these.

TRADITIONAL ENGLISH BLESSING

Dance as though no one is watching you,
Love as though you have never been hurt before,
Sing as though no one can hear you,
Live as though heaven is on earth.

ANONYMOUS

May you be filled with loving kindness.

May you be well.

May you be peaceful and at ease.

May you be happy.

ANCIENT TIBETAN BUDDHIST BLESSING

Do not seek too much fame,

But do not seek obscurity.

Be proud,

But do not remind the world of your deeds.

Excel when you must,

But do not excel the world.

Many heroes are not yet born,

Many have already died.

To be alive to hear this song is a victory.

WEST AFRICAN SONG

––––––––––

When you arise in the morning, give thanks for

the morning light, for your life and strength.

Give thanks for your food and the joy of living.

If you see no reason for giving thanks, the fault

lies in yourself.

TECUMSEH (1768–1813),
CHIEF OF THE SHAWNEE NATION, *GIVE THANKS*

Lord,

Bless the food on our table.

Keep us healthy,

Strong and able.

MARGARET KENNEDY (1896–1967),
AMERICAN POET AND WRITER

Lord, I do give Thee thanks,

For the abundance that is mine.

Today is here.

ANONYMOUS

Hark to the chimes,
Come bow thy head,
We thank Thee, Lord,
For this good bread.

CHIMES GRACE, ANONYMOUS

———————

Gratitude takes three forms:
A feeling in the heart, an expression in words,
and a giving in return.

ARABIC PROVERB

———————

All shall be well,
And all shall be well,
And all manner of thing shall be well.

DAME JULIAN OF NORWICH
(CIRCA 1342–1416), ENGLISH MYSTIC

What is patriotism but a love
of the good things we ate in our childhood?

LIN YÜ-T`ANG (1895–1976),
CHINESE PHILOSOPHER AND POET

Let me smile with the wise and feed with the rich.

DR. SAMUEL JOHNSON (1709–1784),
ENGLISH AUTHOR, LEXICOGRAPHER,
AND CONVERSATIONALIST

––––––––––––––

On such an occasion as this,

All time and nonsense scorning,

Nothing shall come amiss,

And we won't go home til morning.

JOHN BALDWIN BUCKSTONE (1802–1879),
ENGLISH COMEDIAN AND PLAYWRIGHT

––––––––––––––

Lord, for this food make us truly thankful, Amen.

TRADITIONAL BLESSING

Truly now,

Double thanks, triple thanks,

That we've been formed,

We've been given our mouths, our faces,

We speak, we listen, we wonder, we move,

Our knowledge is good,

We've understood what it is for,

We hear and we've seen

What is great and small,

Under the sky and on the earth.

MAYAN BLESSING FROM *POPUL VUH*,
SACRED BOOK OF QUICHE MAYA,
GUATEMALA, CIRCA 600 B.C.

103

May we walk with grace, and
May the light of the universe
Shine upon our path.

ANONYMOUS

O Lord, that lends me life, Lend me a heart
replete with thankfulness.

WILLIAM SHAKESPEARE (1564–1616),
ENGLISH WRITER

Thankfulness sets in motion a chain reaction
that transforms all around us—including
ourselves. For no one ever misunderstands
the melody of a grateful heart. Its message
is universal; its lyrics transcend all earthly
barriers; its music touches the heavens.

ANONYMOUS

It is not the quantity of meat, but the cheerfulness
of the guests which makes the feast.

EDWARD HYDE, EARL OF CLARENDON
(1609–1674), ENGLISH STATESMAN
AND HISTORIAN

O Lord God, heavenly Father, bless us
and these Thy gifts, which we shall accept
from Thy tender goodness. Give us food
and drink. Also for our souls unto life
eternal, and make us partakers of Thy
heavenly table through Jesus Christ.
Amen.

AMISH PRAYER

Joy and gladness shall be found therein,
thanksgiving, and the voice of melody.

ISAIAH, 51:3

It is a good thing to give thanks unto the Lord,
And to sing praises unto Thy name, O most High:
To show forth Thy loving kindness in the morning,
And Thy faithfulness every night.

PSALM 92:1, 2

Thank you very, very much;

My God, thank you.

Give me food today,

Food for my sustenance every day.

Thank you very, very much.

THANKSGIVING PRAYER,
TRADITIONAL SAMBURU
BLESSING, KENYA

Bless this food and us that eats it!

COWBOY GRACE

———————

When we count our many blessings;
It isn't hard to see,
That life's most valued treasures,
Are the treasures that are free.

For it isn't what we own or buy,
That signifies our wealth.
It's the special gifts that have no price:
Our family, friends, and health.

ANONYMOUS, *THE BEST THINGS IN LIFE ARE FREE*

———————

Enter His gates with thanksgiving
And His courts with praise;
Give thanks to Him and praise
His name.

PSALM 100:4

On strawberries:

Doubtless God could have made a better
berry, but doubtless God never did.

WILLIAM BUTLER (1535–1618),
ENGLISH WRITER

Nothing is more graceful than when merriment
possesses all the people, and banqueters listen
in the halls to the singer, sitting in order, and
the tables beside them are filled with bread and
meat, and the wine pourer brings wine decanted
from the bowl and pours it in the cups.

HOMER (CIRCA 700 B.C.), GREEK POET

No ordinary meal—a sacrament awaits us.
On our tables daily spread,
For men are risking lives on sea and land,
That we may dwell in safety and be fed.

SCOTTISH GRACE

O precious food! Delight of the mouth!

O, much better than gold, masterpiece of Apollo!

O flower of all fruits!

O ravishing melon!

MARC-ANTOINE GIRARD, SIEUR DE SAINT-AMANT
(1594–1661), FRENCH POET

All human history attests,

That happiness for men—

The happy sinner!—since Eve ate apples,

Much depends on dinner.

GEORGE GORDON, LORD BYRON
(1788–1824), ENGLISH POET

God be my unfolding,
God be my circle,
God be in my words,
God be in my thoughts.

HEBRIDEAN PRAYER

At this time, O Lord,
We are especially thankful for the golden ripe grain,
And for the hundred kind of red fruits.
Where do they come from? O Lord, they are Thine.

THANKS AT HARVEST, KOREAN BLESSING

It is around the table that friends understand
best the warmth of being together.

ITALIAN SAYING

115

My God, I thank Thee, who hast made

The Earth so bright,

So full of splendor and of joy;

Beauty and light!

So many glorious things are here,

Noble and right!

ADELAIDE ANNE PORTER (1825–1864),
AMERICAN WRITER

———————

Bless all the fruits and vegetables that

    grace our planet.

Especially the kumquat, rutabaga, and pomegranate.

ANONYMOUS

———————

For these and all His mercies,

God's holy name be praised and thanked,

Through Jesus Christ our Lord. Amen

REV. ALLAN HOUSE O'NEIL, ST. JOHN'S
EPISCOPAL CHURCH, WEST HARTFORD, CT

We return thanks to our mother, the Earth, which
   sustains us.
We return thanks to the rivers and streams, which
   supply us with water.
We return thanks to all herbs, which furnish
   medicines for the cure of our diseases.
We return thanks to the moon and stars, which have
   given to us their light when the sun was gone.
We return thanks to the sun, which has looked upon
   the Earth with a beneficent eye.
Lastly, we return thanks to the Great Spirit, in
Whom is embodied all goodness, and Who directs
   all things for the good of Her children.

THANKSGIVING PRAYER, IROQUOIS

Salutations! O Merciful God who provides food for the body and soul, you have kindly granted what is spread before us. We thank you. Bless the loving hands that prepared this meal and us who are to enjoy it, please. Homage, homage, homage to thee!

TAMIL PRAYER, MANIKKA VASAHAR
(8TH CENTURY), SOUTHERN INDIA

To the precious Buddha, unsurpassable Teacher,
To the precious Dharma, unsurpassable Refuge,
To the precious Sangha, unsurpassable Guide,
To the three Jewels, the sources of Refuge,
I make this Offering.

TIBETAN BUDDHIST PRAYER

———————

Blessed be.

ANCIENT CELTIC BLESSING